WHAT MAKES A COMMUNITY?

FIRE STATIONS

by Allison Juda

Consultant: Marla Conn, Reading Specialist, Read-Ability

BEARPORT PUBLISHING

Minneapolis, Minnesota

Teaching Tips

Before Reading

- Look at the cover of the book. Discuss the picture and the title.
- Ask readers to brainstorm a list of what they already know about the fire station. What can they expect to see in this book?
- Go on a picture walk, looking through the pictures to discuss vocabulary and make predictions about the text.

During Reading

- Read for purpose. Encourage readers to think about the fire station and its role in the community as they are reading.
- Ask readers to think about the setting of the book. Where does the story take place?
- Ask readers to look for the details of the story. What is happening?
- If readers encounter an unknown word, ask them to look at the sounds in the word. Then, ask them to look at the rest of the page. Are there any clues to help them understand?

After Reading

- Encourage readers to pick a buddy and reread the book together.
- Ask readers to name three things from this book that they could find at a fire station. Go back and find the pages that tell about these things.
- Ask readers to write and draw a picture about something that they learned about the fire station.

Credits:
Cover and title page, © TennesseePhotographer/iStock; 3, © Valerie Loiseleux/iStock; 5, © martin-dm/iStock; 7, © Rich Koele/Shutterstock; 8, © Fotocrisis/Shutterstock; 9, © Waupee/Dreamstime; 10, © worradirek/Shutterstock; 13, © Brian Vander Brug/Getty Images; 15, © Monkey Business Images/Shutterstock; 16, © Hum Images/Alamy; 17, © BRPH/iStock; 19, © Maskot/Getty Images; 21, © Nancy G Fire Photography, Nancy Greifenhagen/Alamy; 22, © LPETTET/iStock; 23BL, © cmcderm1/iStock; 23TL, © 3D Vector/Shutterstock; 23BR, © BRPH/iStock

Library of Congress Cataloging-in-Publication Data

Names: Juda, Allison, 1993– author.
Title: Fire stations / by Allison Juda ; consultant, Marla Conn.
Description: Minneapolis, Minnesota : Bearport Publishing Company, [2021] |
Series: What makes a community? | Includes bibliographical references
and index.
Identifiers: LCCN 2020029817 (print) | LCCN 2020029818 (ebook) | ISBN
9781647474447 (library binding) | ISBN 9781647474522 (paperback) | ISBN
9781647474607 (ebook)
Subjects: LCSH: Fire stations—Juvenile literature. | Fire extinction—Juvenile literature.
Classification: LCC TH9148 .J83 2021 (print) | LCC TH9148 (ebook) | DDC
628.9/25—dc23
LC record available at https://lccn.loc.gov/2020029817
LC ebook record available at https://lccn.loc.gov/2020029818

For more information, write to Bearport Publishing, 5357 Penn Avenue South, Minneapolis, MN 55419.

Printed in the United States of America.

Contents

A Visit to the Fire Station 4

At the Fire Station 22

Glossary 23

Index 24

Read More 24

Learn More Online.......................... 24

About the Author 24

A Visit to the Fire Station

Today is a big day.

Let's visit the fire station.

We will see where firefighters work.

This is the fire station!

It has big doors in front.

There is something red inside.

FIRE STATION
4

Let's go in.

Look at the huge, red fire truck!

Hard **helmets** hang on the wall.

There are firefighter clothes, too.

Ten House
OVERALL HEIGHT 10'-10"
"STILL STANDING"
FL13002
F.D.
N.Y.
FERRARA
10

There is a lot to do at the fire station.

Some firefighters are training.

They learn how to stay safe.

The fire station has a gym.

Firefighters go to the gym to get strong.

They need to be **healthy**.

20 KG
VOIT
VOIT

Firefighters work and learn at the fire station.

But that is not all!

Sometimes firefighters eat and sleep there, too.

The fire station has a **kitchen**.

Firefighters cook there.

The station also has beds.

Firefighters can sleep when no one needs help.

A loud **alarm** goes off.

This tells the firefighters that someone needs help.

Hurry!

Firefighters put on their helmets and clothes.

They drive off in their fire truck.

125
51
114
125
87

That was a great visit!

The fire station is a busy place.

Do you want to work at a fire station one day?

MENOMONEE
FALLS
115
FIRE DEPT

At the Fire Station

Glossary

alarm something with a bell or buzzer that warns people of something

healthy well and fit

helmets hard hats worn to keep people's heads safe

kitchen a place where food is made

Index

alarm 18
beds 16
fire truck 8, 18, 22
gym 12
helmet 8, 18, 22
kitchen 16

Read More

Donner, Erica. *Fire Station (Around Town).* Minneapolis: Jump! 2018.

Roberts, Antonia. *Firefighters (What Makes a Community?).* Minneapolis: Bearport, 2021.

Learn More Online

1. Go to **www.factsurfer.com**
2. Enter "**Fire Stations Community**" into the search box.
3. Click on the cover of this book to see a list of websites.

About the Author

Allison Juda's uncle was a brave firefighter.
This book is for Robert Fowler.